LAPIS

Also by Kerri Webster

The Trailhead (2018)
Grand & Arsenal (2012)
We Do Not Eat Our Hearts Alone (2005)

LAPIS

Kerri Webster

Wesleyan University Press
Middletown, Connecticut

Wesleyan University Press

Middletown CT 06459

www.wesleyan.edu/wespress

2022 © Kerri Webster

All rights reserved

Manufactured in the United States of America

Designed and typeset in Adobe Jenson Pro

by Eric M. Brooks

Library of Congress Cataloging-in-Publication Data

NAMES: Webster, Kerri, 1971– author.

TITLE: Lapis / Kerri Webster.

DESCRIPTION: First edition. | Middletown, Connecticut:
    Wesleyan University Press, 2022. | Series: Wesleyan poetry |
    Summary: "With meditative and intimate lyrics born in
    the wake of loss, *Lapis* engages themes of genealogy, shared
    histories, and grief"— Provided by publisher.

IDENTIFIERS: LCCN 2022008046 (print) |
    LCCN 2022008047 (ebook) | ISBN 9780819500076 (hardcover) |
    ISBN 9780819500083 (paperback) | ISBN 9780819500212 (ebook)

SUBJECTS: LCGFT: Poetry.

CLASSIFICATION: LCC PS3623.E3974 L37 2022 (print) |
    LCC PS3623.E3974 (ebook) | DDC 811/.6 — dc23/eng/20220225

LC record available at https://lccn.loc.gov/2022008046

LC ebook record available at https://lccn.loc.gov/2022008047

5 4 3 2 1

For
Marni Ludwig
(1976–2019)
and
Jane Mead
(1958–2019)

What I meant when I said "soul"
Was that there should be a place.
JANE MEAD

Where there is sorrow there is holy ground.
OSCAR WILDE

I believe that beautiful unpredictable things will happen again,
for sure. I just think it's going to be a long while.
MARNI LUDWIG

Separate the blue parts, and reduce them, on a piece of
porphyry, to an impalpable powder, which besprinkle with
linseed oil, then make a paste of equal parts of yellow wax, pine
resin, and colophonium, say, 8 oz. of each; and add to this paste
½ oz. of linseed oil, 2 oz. of oil of turpentine, and as much
more mastic. Then take 4 parts of this mixture, and 1 of lapis
lazuli, ground with oil on a piece of porphyry, mix the whole
warm, and suffer it to digest for a month, at the end of which
knead the mixture thoroughly in warm water, till the blue part
separates from it, and at the end of some days decant the liquor.
This ultramarine is exceedingly beautiful.
HENRY HARTSHORNE, *The Household Cyclopedia of
General Information* (1881)

Contents

LAPIS

oh each poet's a / beautiful human girl who must die

and then where do her words go? In the mouth mine feel all wrong, like *ventifact* which means stone planed by aeolian winds into daggered facets but sounds like a furnace part. What's the monosyllable for griefborn lunacy? I dream a festival at which I've forgotten all my verses. I own a dead man's ventifact brutalized by Arctic winds into an awl. Marni was there, standing against the back wall. Someone said the words are under the smoothest stones. Someone said the dictionary shares our beds. Said words reside inside the star-shaped creature. Said words are righteous and come in tongues. Said the Word is broken. Said Broken Thorn Sweet Blackberry. Said the very word is like a bell. Said words alter in our digestive tracts. And someone said the words are numinous, so why can't I see them? Not the words on our shelves, but the ones they didn't get to. What must I leave on the altar of grief to hear their untongued words? A ram? A forest? I will burn this life down to riverbed, will drown in the dead's bitter wine. Silences crush my chest. I don't recall how "The Dead" ends, just remember it as flawless text. What else do I forget? When our mother was dying, my sister said *Get her voice. Get her grocery lists.* I do, I do feel the pull of divesting of the earthly plane. When my mother died, Marni said *Throw that morphine away.* Yum lavender seeping up the plunger. Kingdom Unsaid.

I

Primrose, Orchid, Datura

To say I lived on honeycomb is not enough. I lived
on milkfat, garnets, whiskey bottles under the bed,
lotion pearlescent on pink skin. I slept half the day,
woke late, ate ridiculous bouquets, milked austerity
for gorgeousness — blossoms collected in jars,
granite thieved from silt. I napped and architected
a decadent inwardness. I did not know that the Christbody
would take up residence in the next room, in a hospice
bed, until the whole house smelled like nightblown
Gethsemane, or that this would go on until the world
ran out of sponges from its acrid seas. Once I was a girl
who wore feathers and ivory, a woman who let
the tap run in the desert past all decency. Forgive me.

Seer Stone

Put the stone in the upturned hat. Lean your face into the darkness.
Tell me if the body of Christ can save you, and where the treasure is,
and when the locusts. Tell me if my mother can see her children from
the ether. Two of us are stoned, one of us is drunk, one yells something
across the house to the girlchild who, in being born, saved her.

The first time Joseph Smith encountered a seer stone may have been in the
possession of one Sally Chase. In 1873, Lorenzo Saunders remembered:
*Willard Chase claimed his sister Sally had a peep stone. The Lord bless you
I have seen her peep stone a hundred times; It was a little bit of a stone & it
was green & she would hold it before light.*

The first trial was sleeplessness, tongue heavy in her head heard the dog
call out her name.

The second trial was homeliness, a great power though it takes a while
to learn so.

The third trial was ignorance of the ancestors, specifically that she knew them back only to the -greats, the women who gathered around her bed with faces inconclusive as sand swept across the wood floor.

There is nothing simple about having your soul reduced to a hole between your legs as the men clear the ancient forest and come home fevered. Easy, in that absence, to become a burnt-over girl. Pollen massing in the trees.

In the month after my mother died, I pushed the plunger on the droppers of alprazolam nightly into my mouth as I had pushed them into her mouth, and so was sustained.

For my ancestor Levi, his prophet who is not my prophet meted out this patriarchal blessing in 1835: *You are a strange kind of man. Curious spirits trouble you, but in the name of the Lord Jesus we rebuke all the evil spirits and say to you that you shall overcome them. You shall have a peculiar gift to speak in other tongues.*

Year of:

how long have I been asleep
what has transpired
why

I drive by the cemetery, shout glad news to the dead. The vases flood with rainwater. My mother's buried here a few yards from her sister.

To be secular is ostensibly to be ritual-starved, and yet how many times have I seen a woman manifest a ceremony for a given occasion? Bonfire of burned skirts, prayers scratched into walls, altars assembled in cupboards.

Put the stone in the upturned hat. Lean your face into the darkness.

Having put off grief for the sake of corporeal productivity, finally I attend my mother's grave.

Of another ancestor: *When he was on his mission in 1836 he administered to a man possessed of devils. It took many men to hold the man down. When he opened the door into his room the room seemed filled with evil spirits. He laid his hands on him and commanded the evil spirits to depart; but there seemed to be too much opposition in the room, so he sent out part of the men, and administered again. The devil departed and the man was left limp.*

There is reason to think women in early Mormon history anointed, healed, cast out, but this is not recorded in the family records, nor are matriarchal blessings, nor are the women's conversion narratives.

Here is my new dendritic agate, shape of an egg, white with black markings.

Have you ever kissed a dead woman on the forehead?

Year of:

how long have I been alive
what has transpired
why

To be without a stone in my pocket would frighten me. When I lived away from the sagebrush desert my family came to in 1861, calling holy what had been holy for millennia before their intrusion, I carried a smooth river stone. I would touch it and smell water, taste my lover's skin, see lightning strike the foothills and feel the conflagration, sweating in my sleep.

Mercy
Tyresha
Cynthia
Ida
Permelia
Louisa
Celestia
Martha
Amy
Zelpha
September
Ivy
Sibbilath
Modesty
Sidse
Zillah
Patricia
and on.

Two women, in separate instances, each blessed and healed a child in her care. Neither of these women had ever discussed the blessing with anyone before for fear it would be considered "inappropriate." Another woman gathered her sister's frail, cancer-ridden body in her arms and blessed her with one pain-free day. Several women blessed a close friend just prior to her hysterectomy. One daughter told of a blessing administered to her by her mother for the relief of intense menstrual cramps. Others asked that their experience not be mentioned — again fearing that what had been personal and sacred to them would be misunderstood and viewed as inappropriate by others.

Early on, their prophet said there was a seeing stone for every person on earth waiting to be found, a sort of true love you'd know when you beheld it.

In May my mother decided not to get out of bed again, her lungs two oil slicks. What seemed like a sudden decision was, looking back, her waiting for the academic year to end so that I could be there to administer the doses, arrange the pillows, watch her mind go. This took four months, time out of time, time outside of language, time both sides of the veil, and when it was done every cell in my body was transfigured. I will never again be that exhausted. I will never again be that God-struck.

The Lord bless you before light. I spend a fair measure of time these days talking to the dead. Sometimes all I have to do is roll my eyes.

Put the stone in the upturned hat. Lean your face into the darkness. Show me what megafauna walked the desert, then tell me if the body of Christ can save you, then ask my mother how long to bake this chicken. There are things I need to know. I am scanning the banks for stones.

Against Shame

Nights I walk / and repeat / for myself the prayer / against shame I copied down.
MARNI LUDWIG, "Expert on Shadows"

For the scroll of lamentations, no remedy. Your ravaged arms, your garnet light, your *when*, not *if*: *poison* mistranslated as *honey*. Your words, poet, in my belly. Last night I vomited in the wastebasket. To delay relaying the news of your passing, I counted things screaming in the trees. After the dread duty is fulfilled, may I report: the wages of sin is death, the wages of dying is love, the wages of love is this waking, light striping the walls to which bees are pinned. What have I allowed to rot, stink, fester? I cannot build anything through rhetoric, cannot persuade/dissuade. After the dread duty, sapped of vitality, lapsed into abnegation (sleeplessness. celibacy. eye-motes) for days thinking I'd best rise/call forth some waters/wash the stinking bedding. Forsythia gone bawdy, I swap agency for Claritin, ignore all miracles. And if I say that love holds the property of aseity, will you even believe me? I come from a tabernacled people. *A bird got in my blood*, you wrote. Then the bird killed you with its hundred dollar a day fluttering. I am not who I was.

Relic Hall

Off Swan Falls Road, the deer boneyard, the soiled blanket used to wrap the doe draining to lavender.

Someone has a box of cotton and lightning and it kills them.

Someone has a pad of scribbled night dreams and it doesn't save them.

Born on the date two of my great-great-grandmothers died, wondering which I am or if I'm some sort of Zillah-Ellen hybrid.

The hoof not bone but keratin and fur, and stinks —

"Writing down my foolish name upon the sea" / the names my name contains . . .

Disassembled spine in my car trunk.

You there. I am dead and you are reading this?

A sea of sunset dahlias.

Visitation

Light! Light! I hear her calling when she's a block away as if she's a monger of light. She kneels at my feet, says *I see you've been wallowing, it smells like salt in here.* Well I've lost so many and my dead women call out as I sleep: *Rise and shine.* She comes to the door bearing light like a grief doula. *Get up,* she says, *or I'll command this demon steal your every bright thing.* I get up and she commences a lecture on egg structure, how the only part she'll eat is the chalaza: not the albumen, not the yolk, not the vitelline membrane and not the germinal disc. I tell her I'm going to name my lost child Vitelline and she nods like she already knew that, then gives me a lozenge of light that smells of rosehips and tastes like radial mercy. The sagebrush goes peak bloom and my nightstand's full of antihistamines, the day kind and the night kind. She comes, her adipose cells swollen with light, says *Why don't we scream the names of your dead while tearing our hair out inside an insipid weather of self-pity, then replace the hair with follicles of light,* which feels good (the tearing) though I see how it could become maladaptive. A cloud gathers itself at the end of the street: cumulonimbus. *Close your eyes,* I say to the dead, and she says *Silly they don't need eyes anymore, they see just fine.* She sews fuses under my skin.

It Is an Old Story but One That Can Still Be Told
(Gilgamesh)

On the one hand, it's true that the gods got together on the banks
of the Euphrates and settled on the notion
of being as cruel as possible, on water

as medium for their cruelty. One of them
came to my house as wind bent the locust trees
and let me know the lay of the land, which was
soon-to-be-submerged, as in
You will lose nearly everything, you will go

dispossessed over the barren everywhere.

On the other hand, this is not on balance
the story of that; this is the story of ordinary
bodies in relation to each other, and of those bodies it plainly
says: *It is the story*
of their becoming human together.

And Made My Body an Instrument of the Reckoning

i. The ice in the bowl broken up with the bootheel

ii. The bodily sickness following the emptying of the womb

iii. The hallucinated desert; the tumbleweed glowing; the bones shed; yarrow split through the bones

iv. The plentitude of onions fallen from the truck onto the highway, gathered

v. The vision of Christ wombed and heavy

vi. Dabbling in earthly love, the renunciation of earthly love, the revelation of grief as moth that drinks from our sleeping eyes

vii. The apparition of the friend

viii. The possibility of arriving at a new dispensation outside time yet not outside providence

ix. The inscrutable parable of the onion broth

x. The days of sleep the curtains drawn

xi. Real rabbit hair suspended in false quartz

xii. The citizen activism of the dead

xiii. The refusal of the women to bear the cries of the world; the bafflement of the men in search of succor, as seen through the grown man now at the woman's teat now at the sow's

xiv. The time into arc of the star altitude curves, particularly Arcturus, Caph, Procyon, Denaph, and Caph again

xv. The hawk who grabs the small dog's head, crafting a permanent concavity that in no way lessens the contentment of the dog

xvi. The wearing of hylozoic amulets on which has been spent rent money; the pawning of devices; the many crosses in the vitrine or are they keys

xvii. The stubborn tooth excised from the mouth, blood-pulp affixed; the question of ownership as unrelated to the question of provenance

xviii. Somatism as worldview

xix. The women shaking / the women holding their heads in their hands

xx. *All Being is Being of God and is good: Sin is no Being*

xxi. The tooth mailed priority to a new possessor

xxii. The perfection of the body as seen in the cool forehead of the dead woman

xxiii. The ice in the bowl re-formed

xxiv. The Doctrine of Nonlinear Revelation

xxv. The seizures of the sleeping dog

xxvi. The onion soup esteemed regardless

xxvii. Through agitation, the fibers become a new garment

xxviii. *Wherever the water stands, whatever is inside the star*

xxix. The country called Air Hunger, the country called Vinegar

The New Dispensation

I never wanted to be a mountaineer but so asked the world and so my corsage of pinecones, my conception of the righteous names of love as inclusive of Torn Dead Hare and What Bulb Flowers Survived the Runoff, Chiefly Irises. Having arrived at a place outside the received forms; having deaccessioned the antler I gave to the university, not trusting the institution to caretake beauty; having seen that fatalism is the absence of grace, absence of the belief in grace — I lay down in the dry riverbed. Once I was fond of empirical knowledge and so in a book on my shelves a tiny rosette, a page smeared with fish scales, a page thick with menstrual blood. Wildfire particulates settle in my cervix. My devices fail, the failing a likeable bower. The dead add things to the grocery list, specifically vitamins and while they're well-meaning I don't always do what they say, I use my own judgement. They ask *Were you there when they crucified my Lord* and I say *No but I've seen his body since in the dog spoon-fed antifreeze and, of course, in you all at the end of your days.* Wind lifts the orchid's petals. The riverbed was warm, and I could feel in my hips the ghost river there before water was diverted to the fields. The dead say *How does that make you feel* and I say *Ooh sometimes it causes me to tremble, tremble, tremble, tremble, tremble.*

This Must Be What Happened (Gilgamesh)

I bound red bricks to my feet, lowered into the river.
Lilies eddied pink and sweet
and I grabbed one, and it sliced
my palm, and blood trickled into the water.
I cut the bricks loose from my feet,
kicked back to the bank.
And said to the dead: Look, the lily of resurrection!
I set the plant on the rocks beside my towel.
But then this monster of a universe
got a whiff of pollen
and rose from the water
and ate the goddamned lily!

State of the Union

We let the men speak because their voices soothe them. I grow mercenary and wonder: must I, by the end of this life, go further inland? *Esto perpetua* sings the magpie. I dream Plan B vending machines. A song runs through my head:

> Oh we are done with mildness
> the city burns behind us
> cha cha cha

My heart stacks its yellows up against my will (heliodor, school bus, canary). A command: *To watch, hasten the almond tree flowering early*. The young women ask where I got my authority. They ask three different times, in three different ways. Well, I say, a good many beloveds died. For months I lay down in the wilderness. A man stood in my front yard yelling *bitch* as loud as he could until cops came. Ergo I have far more authority than others, but far less than some. Near here, women were teargassed in the streets, bathing each other's eyes in milk until the Walgreens ran out. My amygdala a companion which, through constancy, has been brought to heel. I used to dream much louder apocalypses. What from the soil has gotten into the plums.

The Dead Teach Me Grounding Techniques

Put a pebble in your shoe. Slit the deer.
Open the gate to the mountains. The asphalt
has begun to pray. Snap a rubber band
around the wrist. Bite the rind. Strip
needles from the pine. Swaddle the wolf.
Place your palm above the flame. Inside
the light. To not go. Swallow the squid
whole. Flagellate. Open the door
to the river. Paint your nipples chartreuse.
Squint until the headstones blur. Step
on a lightbulb. Worry the stone.
Rub in the stain. To remain.
Open the hatch to the sea. Scald
a thumbnail. *Be still.* Let the bee sting.
O clap your hands. Gnash incisors. Bury
your face in fur. *Be not far from me.*

Split

I spend hours talking to a live man. We sit on his bed. I do not tell him about the lark mirror newly arrived from Malta. He disapproves of ornicide — not for food, not for sacrifice. I mean to make lark stew.

There is a dead woman sitting on his dresser and a dead woman trying to get the toilet to stop running, a dead woman drinking the sweet wine in the fridge and a dead woman petting his pacing dachshund. I brought the women with me; — rather, they followed.

They suck their teeth.

He is in the static realm. Not for beauty would he razor a bird's breast.

The lark mirror is mechanical! Twist the dial and the wooden decoy, studded with faceted glass, spins.

Who wouldn't want a little silver music.

We talk and talk. My attention drifts. His hand on my thigh feels like busywork. My dead aunt says *Leave this place and sneak into a hotel swimming pool. Nap. Make a necklace of seed beads.*

It will be work, defeathering a baker's dozen of larks. When we bite — light dribbling down our chins; taste of iron nails.

Oh My Darlings

I would love you ten years before the flood
and would not, for any portion of those years,
make ready. Let the waters, let
the brine, rain a premonition
as what, finally,

                      isn't: not quince. Not the dog
inside his whimper. I am in a strange sea
that smells of juniper, I take my
punishment, want

harder, force the quince in hot water, rest

until the sutures have collapsed, worlds
fallen in, gap between my palm and the small
of the back more wet than I remembered.
The sea people want to be the land people.
Tourmaline as death-cheat: a cabinetful
of things on chains.

And so it came to pass that time was only a tent
we might unzip and crawl out from.
And there by the lake of burnt and silver trees
    I vowed *Hurt me.*
    And the world said *How would you like it.*

To do without / to wait / to study / to punish / to work
until pleasure: I fail at the museum, I fail
in the garden, I fail and then
I weep and then
I open the book again.
I hold your hand. I oblate. Iron
bowl lined with gold, eyes
cloudy, humidifier chugging —
I will votive you until the sea itself is lit.
I will wrap wire around the leaves
so that when the leaves dissolve
I will still have the wire.

The weeping and
the peppermint;
the sound
of the breathing tank.

I Go and See a Man About Some Lapis

I made of my sadness a lanyard
I made of my sadness a tomb
Little owl, I said to my sadness, get disemboweling

I purchase a sterling dodo the size of my thumb.
I purchase fool's gold and I purchase gilded loam
in the shape of a man and I give him
ALL my painted clay and he eats it.
I do not know what to do with this ivory goat, inherited, full udders
grazing my nightstand.

I made of my sadness a comet
I made of my sadness an albatross / *Look what I'm wearing*
My sadness a gilded womb
and what I pushed out —

I double down on investing in our folly.
I go and see a man about some lapis.
We circle each other.
He is reluctant to divest of his supply.
I only want a morsel.
I have oak gall at the ready. Have the loveliest pestle.

The highest grade powder, pyrite impurities lifted out
with a magnet,
sells for fifty grand a kilo.
He says *I covet my lapis.*
I say *I covet my dead and there are things I need to write them*
that require ultramarine or
they won't be able to read it.
I say: *It's what I need to get well, to get right*
in the head, to get right with my dead. Just a taste.
To rub on my gums.
To touch to their hems.

So Many Worlds, So Much to Do

For three days I had a fever
and when I woke I saw the
shapes of things. My funny
privy council.

A word came to me secretly.

There is a soul in my locket.

I *watch and hasten* but what
surfaces proves no anodyne.
Having given my calling the
fullest obedience and rarely
made passive my mouth
sounds — the Furies unseen
on the trailhead for months —
my hands slick with the
scales of gutted trout — *Why
should our translation say
"grasshoppers." Locusts is the
word; & the figure is incomplete
without it.*

Too many souls in this
bed. I shove them out with
the pads of my feet. The
strawberries macerate in
their bowl. Of God I ask
an emptiness which does
not come. There is vigilance
and there is vigil and every
woman must learn to parse.

The dead say *Are you trying
to save someone again.* No. On
the striped body of Christ
I swear I am not. *Then why
aren't you sleeping. Why aren't
you eating.* I don't want to be
this new species.

And aren't the graves
humming. And haven't
I ground my teeth down
to nothing. And didn't
I bring the sweet spices.
And didn't I bring the
sweet oil.

The dead say things they
said when they were alive,
*Going to curl up with the
dog / tried to hang a curtain
rod but it wouldn't go into the
wall.*

A bad day, reverse-
ambulatory.

I feared she was going to die
when she wrote *Poetry has
betrayed me.* The children
play Pioneer, stomachs full
of deer. *God bless! God bless!*
chirps the worrybird. *I believe
in the dust and the grasses.* In
the stockyards and most of
what seems real. I make stew;
I drink light from a brass
bowl; bark grows around the
wound, bark is clever?

To exist in a physical world:
a parliament of women /
figs and candles for them /
figs and candles

On each planet a single shack
soldered from scrap, the
rain percussive and brilliant:
that's where the dead are? In
the other room, aides pace
the House floor between
hearings: this is television and
real as any owl or radio. A
temple slides into the sea.

I didn't want to enter the
shacks. Didn't want to —

And all the while a busy
household full of comings,
goings, debts. HOW do I
name an animal under these
circumstances, WHAT does
the muse want from me,
WHERE did the lover get off
saying obsidian is common,
so is fire. Say the stone is
apotropaic. Say the pill is.
I can pretend to believe
anything. The barometric
pressure plummets. And an
army of women moves over
the earth, wiping the brows
of the dying.

Having seen that fatalism is
the absence of grace, of the
belief in grace — was grace
dissolved the shoulder clot,
and grace that brings us the
pre-dead. For the privilege of
full-snotted keening. *Our little
systems have their day.* The
dead say nothing is singular,
there is a new dispensation,
get ready. The lilies evolve into
sentience.

Sleep-weary and the shapes
keep up their shifting. I
know a man forbidden by
writ of law to cross the river,
yet the body does not work
that way, even if we put
bands of silver between the
stanzas.

The locket has a porthole
window. Soul's chewing
pollen in there. Even in the
grand after, the world is
transported on a bee's ass.

Soul says *Notalone is the worst*
pun / says *Pull it together*
woman / says *Outta here like*
Vladimir / says *Don't get lippy*
with me missy / says *We're*
in business, we're in business.
What the dead women want
is revolution, they want
what they wanted when
they were alive, only harder;
pragmatists, and they know
I'm praying for a lustrum, a
lustrum, our kingdom for a
lustrum: and they pray with
and for me: and coo, sure, but
cooing only gets a gal so far.

Once emerged from the gray
of night, which is composed
of smoke, we see that a new
dispensation is upon us. I
place my palms flat on the
poems of the dying / tremble
from the current / exit
wired: wine poured off the
footbridge wine on your
strange feet —

A rock. A vibration of light.
Let rum be the last thing I
taste. Or plums? Or ink? A
man drives drunk into the
cemetery; the dead tut-tut;
groundskeepers right the
toppled graves. Don't put
me here. Oh don't I fail and
fail and fail at being / doing
well. Who made the lace?
Who made the lapis vault?
The birds chirp-chirp from
shoeboxes their tender, tender
eternities.

And if you think a body can't
be its own psychopomp, well.

Saturnalia coming on. I
let Soul out and it hums
along the house's wiring.
Resuming my place as a
woman of action, I plan
the colloquium, my body
at this altered desk not at
this desk [the book of the
dead beside the book of
the living / a coyote's jaw to
devour the law / slag from
the glassblower's floor / three
figs]. The colloquium will
be informative and shabbily
catered.

I now recognize myself, says
the Chairman, throat filled
with static. This new gray
hair coarser than my previous
hair, maybe a bald spot — ?
To stay bodied, I build
advents for the living and
advents for the dead, twenty-
five small tins with things
like scripture and glow in the
dark cats.

I knew my failings required a
thousand offerings, knew that
cruelty was what rendered
sacrifice a sacrifice. Serum
said everyone. Serum said the
radio.

Lapis lodged in gums:
that's how we know women
lettered the holy texts. What
comes before the doctrine of
spots of time is a drowned
body; what comes after is a
hanged body. I am building
a house for the dead, I am
speaking only for myself,
wrestling with sleep as
though it were a dread
machine. Warily the animal
sniffs his new bed, rubs his
pheromones all over. Parts
for which I am praying: her
uterus, his freedom, her
circulatory system. I shut the
door so no one knocks but
they still knock.

At the grocery store, Soul
claps its hands and sings, then
louder sings for every tatter in
its mortal dress, says Will you
be my singing-master? Oh. I
can't even learn to walk with
a pebble in my shoe, I can't
make a proper lark stew, I cry
at faculty meetings, I failed
you and would surely fail you
again. We fa la ploddingly
through the ordinary and
then — Sarah calls about the
clot in her shoulder. The dead
women recurse behind her,
but their presence does not
keep my soul from going I
think to Saturn or is it hell.
Just where I fracture to I
cannot say, but I don't like
it there. A spot of time is a
sinkhole, not a prettiness.

*I believe in the dust and the
grasses.* In the stockyards
and most of what seems real.
The greyhound conspires
to fill the Amazon box with
himself. The bee goes sloppy
with gold. And the thinning
of the veil — Knock knock.

Tired of scrubbing blood
from the altar, eventually the
Romans switched to wax
figurines.

The speed of revelation
faster than the speed of
transcription, the gate
to the other world won't
close. The sego lilies are
burning but the bulbs
remain edible. If grief is
transfiguration, what are
we, after?

IV

State of the Union

She manifests the Republic as a rash. Worries that curing it — spiderwort? vinegar? Neosporin? — will render her body falsehood. It's the itching that keeps her from fully becoming a thine, a typewriter, or a Lampad, which is for the best — that she remain — as she is soft to lie upon and not a vase (not prone to shattering; plurality of openings). Despite the pain.

The people foulbrood into the agora, scrape their disease onto the air, shake their red-hatted bodies awkwardly in a way meant to appear as celebration.

The words in her hair say WINGED, LAME, PRODUCED FROM EGGS, LIVING AND DYING ON ALTERNATE DAYS, a working theory of the half-children of God. When she scrapes a bit of shell from the side of the bowl, she remembers,

and fasts to bring on reverie. What if the real, placed inside the poet, makes them "a god of passionate sadness"? A sybil of glistening madness? A demiurge of screwed up gladness? A numen of the house of vastness? Can't she maybe just be a minor magus of hapless apparatus, a zealous gladys? In her cabinet glows the uranium glass.

Of Hutto

The first Hutto woman discovered fire by slamming this rock against that rock with such force the sky became ordinance. Have you ever loved like that? The first woman to bring law to Hutto did so by brushfire. This is called "The Year Law Came by Brushfire." The women of Hutto nurse rabbits with glass droppers. The old men of Hutto recite their feats and dream, touch themselves, turn beside their wives like baby gyres. The clouds above Hutto galleon in homage to corpsed empires. The hanging gardens of Hutto hang from chatelaines. My god the wishlets of Hutto. My god the solar lamps.

Are my dead there in Hutto? Come winter the women of Hutto construct a scale village inside their village wherein the ordinal spirits can rest. The women of Hutto know you can be a son of a bitch but you can't be a son of a gun any more than you can be the son of a flashlight. The arc of history swings above the gate to Hutto like a saw on which is played "Greensleeves" at a pancake breakfast. One Hutto woman sucks a quartz pebble. One answers questions in the form of a question. What is "feeling that way?"

Hutto: Safe at Night!, proclaim the imaginary billboards of Hutto. What is bear spray? What are keys between fingers? What are cat-o'-nine-tails? Someone from Hutto posts an article from Democracy Now even as her Hutto sister hawks a five buck vitamin she swears cures the virus.

The good men of Hutto are extraordinarily tender both in their souls and their soles leaving them vulnerable to slivers ontological and plywood.

The Hutto woman who answers questions in the form of a question is called a smarty pants and a know-it-all, yes, but not a tattletale, gossip, busybody, nosey parker, nag, scold, blabbermouth, chatterbox, windbag, airhead, space case, dingbat, battle-axe, ball-breaker, ball and chain, matron, marm, old bat, old bag, old maid, old biddy, hag, wallflower, Plain Jane, frump, cow, sow, pig, butter face, goody-two-shoes, prude, Miss Prim, cocktease, slut, whore, jezebel, cum bucket, slattern, hussy, trollop, Nervous Nellie, loon, stick-in-the-mud, harpy, virago, or harridan.

The girls of Hutto send their dreams onto the reservoir on boats built from waxed milk cartons; the girls of Hutto are more spirit than Spirit can bear; the girls of Hutto know that neither communions nor intercourses nor sweet sixteens demarcate womanhood and wonder aloud what DOES into the magnificent kelp-flow of each other's hair.

What is outer space to the inner life of the women of Hutto? Hutto bread is not LIKE the son's body, the bread IS the son's body and when you partake he's Gethsemaned all over again and his cries shake the earth and rightly you tremble and rightly you sway and what is sway but a tree standing by the water? The churches of Hutto do what they can knowing they are neither ambulatory nor ambulances.

What is the Praetorian Guard? In whose house lurks the last living landline? In Hutto "primogeniture" is the punchline to every joke and the women snort as they say it, wiping tears from each other's eyes.

Alas Hutto is not sovereign. The detention center called Hutto which is not in Hutto but another part of the state is more sovereign than Hutto or the Holy See because therein man's law has murdered God's.

Let me tell you of the embroidered alphabets of Hutto. The comely rosettes.

The mayor of Hutto decrees it a fineable crime to teach children about similes before puberty. Wishy-washy, she says, and the mothers of Hutto concur. Bothsidesism, she says, and they yep yep. Am I any different than the balsam mobiles that hang above the seated women of Hutto? If forgiveness is an animal, how many eyes does it have? Nervous Nellie stands in the front pew and testifies that if you're not nervous you're stupid, ffs.

Who knows if marriage in Hutto is terrestrial or celestial.

The recording secretary of Hutto says she will no longer concern herself with minutes, has transcended minutes, and with that all of Hutto goes full millennialist. This is called "The Year Hutto Went Full Millennialist."

No, says a Hutto woman, it's Democracy Now!

The oldest woman in Hutto drafts a new Magna Carta inside a tarp tent a mile above town.

Each night I astral project into Hutto, each morning I wake knowing less. What is fair? What is right? A Hutto fox is not LIKE a psalter, a Hutto fox IS a psalter. Are my dead there in Hutto, are their arms tracked, can they breathe, are they classic mirror ghosts who emerge from the mirrors at night. The loneliest girl in Hutto swallows nutmeg till she hallucinates heaven and her shit smells beautiful.

Towards a Discipline of Joy

Each July I go mildly suicidal into the mind's dovecote as the birds sue for their kingdom and loudly. My lost friend said of teaching poetry at Rikers: *I'm not showing up with track marks on my hands. Those women deserve better.*

Sky sick with sun, the man drags the dog along the sidewalk by its collar. The girl carries her brother piggyback, swimsuits dripping as insects hydroplane over the gutter.

Writing about something monstrous, a friend asks, *Is it beautiful enough?*

Here at the midpoint of my life what I wish I had said is, *Wear fingerless gloves.*

Extraordinarily is how the juniper bush flourishes, spilling out into the street, over the street and onto the next lawn.

The Garden as Partition Like the One in Every Annunciation

Once emerged from the gray of night
heavier and dearer and stronger
than the fire of the night
drunk with God and doubled over

Garden as neutered wilderness
Garden as greenshield
Garden as darkened glass
Garden as forcefield

At first he rose from the gray of the night,
then heavy and precious
and made strong by fire
in the evening pervaded by God and bent

Garden as liminal hush
Garden as rabbit hutch
Garden as rainwall
Garden as perforated veil

Having woken from night's ashes
made weighty, burnished
tempered
tipsy with immanence; supplicated

Garden as torture room
Garden as keening green
Garden as just before
Garden as crawling floor

And One Ge·ra·ni·um

I scatter the last of my mother's ashes under the locust trees.
A man I slept with last summer sends lonely heart letters
filled with feathers and clippings that say things like *To understand a man*
you must understand what days mattered to him, and what mattered to Olson . . .
A woman carves a hairpin for my friend; it has her ancestors in it; has the sea.
I read a book which claims men first cleared forests
for a skyhole through which to talk to God.
Some uranium glass gets lost in customs.
This is simple human error.
I maintain that a Wunderkammer is still possible.
Oh Olson all the days.

The Lapis Nuns and the Radium Girls Meet in the Hereafter

And eat ortolans together, the radium girls' jaws
recomposed from shard and God. Feet up,
they watch orogeny pleat the earth. What
they hear in the after: gossip, wind, no
second hand sweeping the dial. *Was it*
worth it is the question: to feel your molar
fall out into your lover's mouth, to scribe the part
where the father creates the son expressly
to fatten then slaughter him, nails shredding
his wrists like boiled chicken? They touch
sponges to each other's lips and coo, suck
goodbitter from the vinegar. Sometimes
the ortolans have vim left in them, flap as they
slide down. A lapis nun shows the radium girls
a fleck of the Christmother's hem lodged
in her gums. A radium girl shows the lapis nuns
the hole in her neck where sky leaks through.
They all agree that earth had something
to do with time, with the division of time into
twelves or sixties or thirty-threes or millennia,
but remembering grows hazy. Aren't we
immortal! they say, and nod. That
was half-life, they say, and this is the other.

Clorox

The bleach burn on the scrubbing hand radiant —
radial — injury emanating from this forced
obedience to fatherland, this imperative
to scrub and scrub, the hand the instrument
of love the likes of which a king goes hard for
even as the redness rises, stings, stays
for days, each time the hand is washed the skin
reagitated, swollen, become more club than fist
until finally the outer layer sloughs off, fresh
skin air-kissed and nothing for it but to pray:
once there were zero chemicals in my pantry,
help me now here I am this day trying not
to breathe, scrubbing down (switches,
knobs, knobs) in unison with the citizenry
this country covered in the shit of ages, past
the top layer of the king's excrement, back
and back through pestilences, wipety wipe,
burnt hand a lame gauzed offering as bleach
saturates the gauze anew and the skin goes
sunburn-slick while the king says his waste
is beautiful and we pat him on the head and
let him doodle with it as the work goes on and on
and it seems the fingers of my hand might web,
become something fit to slide back into the sea,
dread humanness molted. Until then I need milk
and, absent a fog machine, fear the aisles unclean.

I make daiquiris with rum bought to sanitize wounds
plus countertops. If this present is the world's etcetera,
should I make a will? Leave tulips on the doorsteps
of the beloved? Watch the doctors on tv cry, and cry
along? Touch — the only sure comfort — denied us,
I fear someone's manhandled the coffee pot and
dream the world gathers itself on balconies to scoff
at our lame Republic: *We knew they never had it in them.*
Which they do / which we don't. Sagebrush season,
I drive through a town that does not want me there
out to the desert where I kneel, kick rattlesnake skin,
gather bullet casings and obsidian near the lava hill
one can scale to look into the future, scout oncoming
danger. I stay sea-leveled, drive home past rows of pens
too small for cattle to turn around in. At the railroad
crossing, a boy throws quartz pebbles at graffitied cars.
I wait and while I wait I sanitize the steering wheel.

Once we wore silver chains around our waists from
which we hung thermometers in sterling cases, smelling
salts, compacts, sewing needles, buttonhooks, glasses,
pencils, keys, thimbles, knives so small you might've
thought we'd never hurt a fly / a soul. Before chatelaines,
who knows. See the woman there, wiping fever
from a stranger's forehead? Here is a silver walnut
and inside it: straight pins, mirror, powder puff.
Here is a tiny case for holding a bit of sponge
dipped in vinegar to soothe a Christ or ward off
the smell of the dead as you step over Him, here
is a whistle so gorgeously engraved you might
forget there was never a time before danger, here
is your tampon, your Xanax, your Purell, here an aide
memoire so you might write it down and never forget
again. To whom to bequeath my follies, to whom
my worry? If I run out of eyedrops will my eyelids stick
to my corneas, if I run out of Benadryl will I not sleep?
Yes and yes and I want out of the Penetralium
of mystery, survive by obsessive concretizing, terrified
of the spectral essence of words which are only
sounds. All my ladies should take up yodeling and
love in pure phoneme from here on out, reverberations
moving from head voice to chest voice with a grace
that, as we nod across the hills, will summon hooved
animals we did not know were there. Ay ee, ay oo
I have no butter, have you? Oh ah I have butter
but no lard or heroin, and look! the Lamb of God
is nuzzling my palm though from your vantage
he must seem a puffy speck. I think I just murdered
an eon's lichen with my step. Ay oh let's rest —

I dream there's a counter to refresh for past mass
death events and wake soul-sick, slick with sweat
but without fever. Once, in a clinic, a doctor
had me plan the world in twenty-minute increments.
I shave and oil my legs and want a paisley robe.
Is there a counter clicking down the king's hours?
In the Blitz, women filled their dance cards and
screwed away the end of days. I think my hand
is permanently red. I am kneeling in the desert,
am never not kneeling there, the Owyhees floating
in the distance, on boulders glyphs that record
which way the megafauna. Out of limes, I switch
to rum and cokes and learn no useful skill: not
bread making, not embroidery, not trench warfare.
Laze with me. Mistresses, misters, I have tried
to be good, have punished myself by removing
myself, have gone half-corpsed but now see when
the cleaning-fog machines lift their fog — my vanity:
and want what the body wants: an ivory-handled
hairbrush, a gentleman: weary of prognostications
revelations locusts, the locusts scratching these
windows, the antibiotics hoarded. I pre-bequeath
my former righteousness in this handkerchief.

Nothing in my hands I bring: see? The whale
levitates above the field. Memory smears its
ectoplasm. Shoulder to stone, the women roll
the stone back. Could my zeal no respite know?
Lick the ectoplasm off you. Around old growth
tables, they coach and coach but the king cannot
ape humanness. Days thick as petroleum jelly,
the house reeks of bleach and bacon grease. If
I die, oo ee, take from between my breasts this
gold hazelnut which reliable sources contend
is everything that is. Then swallow everything.
If you die, I'll swallow you the way Marni did Jon's
ashes after he OD'd on the kitchen floor. Hear
ye: the mountain of the Lord's house shall be
established at the top of the mountain and at the foot
of the mountain a door and inside the door
a woman picking at the sore on her breast and a dog
licking its mange down to bone and a man who
says the state reads his mind since he returned
from the last lost war, and there, piled in a corner,
the women the Lord made bald for wantonness,
and the singed peeling women from when the Lord
said tinkling instruments said burning instead of
beauty. The bald women make a salve for the burned
women from fiddlehead ferns and spit. Time was
I wanted holiness to be a text read metaphorically
to palliate His cruelty and so was shut from the Lord.
At the still center of the universe, a door, and behind
the door: the hazelnut. Ah and awe the people crowd
the hills. The squirrels are screaming in the trees and in
your eye I see the dead as through a keyhole. Cleft for me.

Elegy

And I *was* equal to my longing:
the mums blackening;
sorrow a carboned figurine;
the firmament steaming; your ashes
interred in the boulder;
the ugly birds crying *dolor dolor dolor*;
the sky smoke-choked — what, then,
would you have had be my register?
As the beasts of the field rub their antlers off
with ooh-itch pleasure; as the screen says
You often open around this time; as the grapes
blight: listen: sometimes
we're the pilgrim, sometimes
we're the site.

Eyelets

Say you're the ram in the thicket, for two seconds
allowed to believe you're free
by a bartering god who alters his actions
yet never once claims his nature has changed.
I am building a bone parure.
There is a type of stone of great renown among the Gauls.
It has a hole
and through the hole comes revelation.
There is energy under the earth waiting to be released.
In abandoned houses, men ravel copper back onto giant spools.
A white stone, and in the stone a new name written.
A hag stone also has a hole; a wishing stone a stripe.
All summer someone I love gathered milk
and went out to meet burning night.
And who will wash our sight.
Who will let us see through the milk veil to another kingdom.
Cauled, from the Latin *galeatum,* meaning helmeted.

Acknowledgments

Colorado Review	"So Many Worlds, So Much to Do"
Guernica	"Visitation"
Image	"Seer Stone"
Los Angeles Review	"The Dead Teach Me Grounding Techniques,"
	"Primrose, Orchid, Datura"
Propeller	"Oh My Darlings"

Notes

The epigraph "What I meant when I said 'soul' / Was that there should be a place" is from Jane Mead's poem "Concerning That Prayer I Cannot Make."

The epigraph "I believe that beautiful unpredictable things will happen again, for sure. I just think it's going to be a long while" was a message from Marni Ludwig on March 18, 2017.

"oh each poet's a / beautiful human girl who must die": The title is from Alice Notley's "World's Bliss."

I
"Primrose, Orchid, Datura": "I lived on honeycomb" comes from Oscar Wilde's *De Profundis.*

"Seer Stone": The italicized passage beginning *"Two women, in separate instances . . ."* is from "The Historical Relationship of Mormon Women and Priesthood," an essay by Linda King Newell in *Dialogue: A Journal of Mormon Thought.* Other passages are taken from family histories as compiled on familysearch.com.

II
"Against Shame": "The scroll of lamentations" is from the book of Isaiah. The line "A bird got in my blood" is Marni Ludwig's, from her poem "Clinic" in the book *Pinwheel.* This poem is for Chris Dennis.

"Relic Hall": "Writing down my foolish name upon the sea" comes from Elizabeth Barrett Browning's *Aurora Leigh.*

"It Is an Old Story but One That Can Still be Told" and "This Must Be What Happened": These poems are translations of Herbert Mason's translation of *Gilgamesh.* "It is the story / of their becoming human together" comes from that text.

"And Made My Body an Instrument of the Reckoning": This poem is based on the table of contents of Julian of Norwich's *Revelations of Divine Love*. "All Being is Being of God and is good: Sin is no Being" comes from that text. "Wherever the water stands, whatever is inside / the star" is Marni Ludwig's, from her poem "Votive."

"The New Dispensation": The poem's ending is taken from the hymn "Were You There When They Crucified My Lord."

"State of the Union": *Esto Perpetua* is the state motto of Idaho. "To watch, hasten the almond tree flowering early" comes from Elizabeth Barrett Browning's Bible marginalia as transcribed by Lisa Fishman in her chapbook *"The Holy Spirit does not deal in synonimes": Notes by Elizabeth Barrett in the Margins of Her Greek and Hebrew Bibles.*

"The Dead Teach Me Grounding Techniques": "Open the gate to the mountain" is from *Gilgamesh*. "Scald a thumbnail" echoes Adrienne Rich's "Snapshots of a Daughter-in-Law." "Be still," "O clap your hands," and "Be not far from me" are from the Psalms.

"Oh My Darlings": "I would love you ten years before the flood" is from Andrew Marvell, "To His Coy Mistress." A version of this poem was originally published as "Varieties of Silence."

III
"So Many Worlds, So Much to Do": The title is Tennyson's, from *In Memoriam*, as is "Our little systems have their day." "A word came to me secretly," "I watch and hasten," "Why should our translation say 'grasshoppers,' Locusts is the word; & the figure is incomplete without it," and "a rock. A vibration of light" are Elizabeth Barrett Browning, from *"The Holy Spirit does not deal in synonimes": Notes by Elizabeth Barrett in the Margins of Her Greek and Hebrew Bibles.* "Tried to hang a curtain rod but it wouldn't go into the wall" and "I fear poetry has betrayed me" are Marni Ludwig's words. "I believe in the dust and the grasses" and "To exist in a physical world" are from Jane Mead. "Once emerged from the gray of night" is the title of a Paul Klee painting.

IV
"State of the Union": "WINGED, LAME, PRODUCED FROM EGGS, LIVING AND DYING ON ALTERNATE DAYS" is Pliny the Elder.

"Of Hutto": This poem owes its genesis to Kathleen Finneran.

"The Garden as Partition Like the One in Every Annunciation": The lines "Once emerged from the gray of night / heavier and dearer and stronger / than the fire of the night / drunk with God and doubled over" are a translation of Paul Klee's lines from his painting *Once Emerged from the Gray of Night*.

"And One Ge♦ra♦ni♦um": The title is from Dickinson 486.

"Clorox": This poem quotes from Isaiah and the hymn "Rock of Ages," and references Julian of Norwich.

"Elegy": The first line echoes Jane Mead's "I am not equal to my longing," from her poem "Concerning That Prayer I Cannot Make."

"Eyelets": The poem quotes Revelations: "He that hath an ear, let him hear what the Spirit saith unto the churches; To him that overcometh will I give to eat of the hidden manna, and will give him a white stone, and in the stone a new name written, which no man knoweth saving he that receiveth it." "There is a type of stone of great renown among the Gauls" is from Lucretius.

Gratitude to Martin Corless-Smith for finding titles in haystacks.

About the Author

Kerri Webster is the author of the poetry collections *The Trailhead*, *Grand & Arsenal* (winner of the Iowa Poetry Prize), and *We Do Not Eat Our Hearts Alone*. The recipient of awards from the Whiting Foundation and the Poetry Society of America, she was a Visiting Writer-in-Residence at Washington University in St. Louis from 2006 to 2010. She currently teaches at Boise State University.